Larger than Life

Northern Dancer
King of the Racetrack

Gare Joyce

Fitzhenry & Whiteside

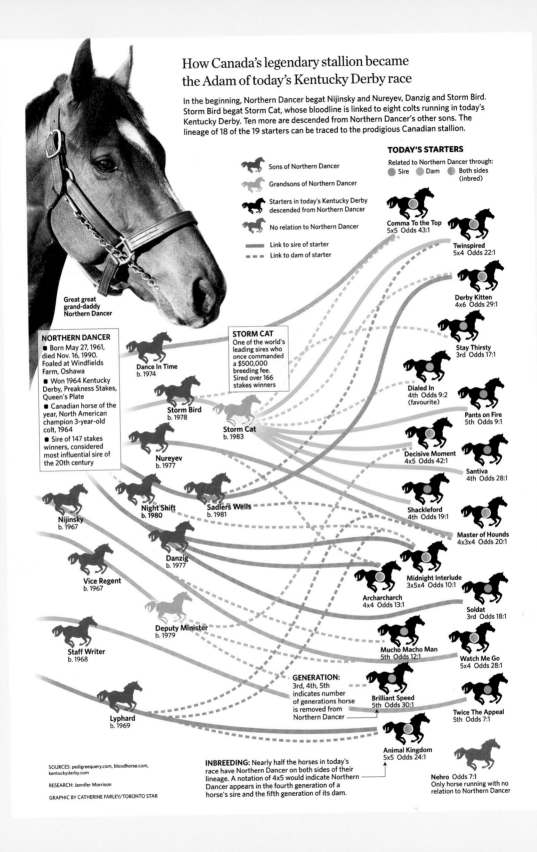

How Canada's legendary stallion became the Adam of today's Kentucky Derby race

In the beginning, Northern Dancer begat Nijinsky and Nureyev, Danzig and Storm Bird. Storm Bird begat Storm Cat, whose bloodline is linked to eight colts running in today's Kentucky Derby. Ten more are descended from Northern Dancer's other sons. The lineage of 18 of the 19 starters can be traced to the prodigious Canadian stallion.

Sons of Northern Dancer

Grandsons of Northern Dancer

Starters in today's Kentucky Derby descended from Northern Dancer

No relation to Northern Dancer

Link to sire of starter

Link to dam of starter

TODAY'S STARTERS

Related to Northern Dancer through:
Sire   Dam   Both sides (inbred)

Great great grand-daddy Northern Dancer

NORTHERN DANCER
- Born May 27, 1961, died Nov. 16, 1990. Foaled at Windfields Farm, Oshawa
- Won 1964 Kentucky Derby, Preakness Stakes, Queen's Plate
- Canadian horse of the year, North American champion 3-year-old colt, 1964
- Sire of 147 stakes winners, considered most influential sire of the 20th century

STORM CAT
One of the world's leading sires who once commanded a $500,000 breeding fee. Sired over 166 stakes winners.

Dance In Time b. 1974

Storm Bird b. 1978

Storm Cat b. 1983

Nureyev b. 1977

Night Shift b. 1980

Sadlers Wells b. 1981

Nijinsky b. 1967

Danzig b. 1977

Vice Regent b. 1967

Deputy Minister b. 1979

Staff Writer b. 1968

Lyphard b. 1969

Comma To the Top 5x5 Odds 43:1

Twinspired 5x4 Odds 22:1

Derby Kitten 4x6 Odds 29:1

Stay Thirsty 3rd Odds 17:1

Dialed In 4th Odds 9:2 (favourite)

Pants on Fire 5th Odds 9:1

Decisive Moment 4x5 Odds 42:1

Santiva 4th Odds 28:1

Shackleford 4th Odds 19:1

Master of Hounds 4x3x4 Odds 20:1

Midnight Interlude 3x5x4 Odds 10:1

Archarcharch 4x4 Odds 13:1

Soldat 3rd Odds 18:1

Mucho Macho Man 5th Odds 12:1

Watch Me Go 5x4 Odds 28:1

Brilliant Speed 5th Odds 30:1

Twice The Appeal 5th Odds 7:1

Animal Kingdom 5x5 Odds 24:1

Nehro Odds 7:1
Only horse running with no relation to Northern Dancer

GENERATION: 3rd, 4th, 5th indicates number of generations horse is removed from Northern Dancer

INBREEDING: Nearly half the horses in today's race have Northern Dancer on both sides of their lineage. A notation of 4x5 would indicate Northern Dancer appears in the fourth generation of a horse's sire and the fifth generation of its dam.

SOURCES: pedigreequery.com, bloodhorse.com, kentuckyderby.com

RESEARCH: Jennifer Morrison

GRAPHIC BY CATHERINE FARLEY/TORONTO STAR

Contents

The Canadian

Northern Dancer, the great Canadian racehorse

He was short. He was chunky. He was plain. He looked funny when he ran. He was all the things that people expect a great athlete *not* to be.

Northern Dancer was a colt born at Windfields Farm in Oshawa, Ontario. He may have been small for a racehorse, but back in 1964 he was the best three-year-old thoroughbred in North America. And that year, Northern Dancer was the biggest newsmaker in the country's sporting scene.

In May 1964, at Churchill Downs racetrack in Louisville, Kentucky, Northern Dancer won the Kentucky Derby—the world's most famous and prestigious horse race. Even more impressive is that he was the first Canadian-bred horse to win the Derby, and he did it in record time! Then, three weeks later, Northern Dancer raced at the Pimlico Race Course in Maryland and won the Preakness Stakes—the "second jewel" of the American Triple Crown of Thoroughbred Racing. The last race in the Triple Crown was the Belmont Stakes in Elmont, New York—where Northern Dancer finished in third place. But his season did not end there: He capped a glorious year by winning the Queen's Plate at Woodbine Racetrack in Toronto, near his hometown.

In one amazing season of racing, Northern Dancer became known as a horse of the people. He was physically unimpressive, frequently underestimated, and had parents whose careers were cut short. But he was a horse with a competitive spirit and a lot of heart, so he was able to outrun a great number of better bred and more imposing horses.

Sports editors voted Northern Dancer into the Canadian Sports Hall of Fame in May 1964, making him the first equine member of the Hall. He was inducted not only because he won many famous races, but also because of his ability to sire

Triple Crown

The Triple Crown refers to a series of three horse races for three-year-old thoroughbred horses run each year. The American Triple Crown—consisting of the Kentucky Derby, the Preakness Stakes, and the Belmont Stakes—is perhaps the most famous of the Triple Crowns. There is also a Canadian Triple Crown which consists of the Queen's Plate, the Prince of Wales Stakes, and the Breeders' Stakes.

A mural of Northern Dancer's life, painted by David Yeats on the side of a building in Oshawa, Ontario

great racehorses, whose decendants continue to become champions. Northern Dancer changed horse racing forever, and experts in thoroughbred racing have said that he was the most important sire of the century.

Northern Dancer made more money as an accomplished racehorse and sire than any Canadian athlete in history—even more than Wayne Gretzky or any other great hockey player. Over the years, hundreds of millions of dollars changed hands because of Northern Dancer. Of course, the legend of Northern Dancer goes beyond money, and this is reflected in the many honours that he has received. Canada Post issued a stamp bearing his picture, and statues stand at racetracks and farms memorializing Northern Dancer. Years after his racing career ended, fans continue to travel from as far away as Europe and Japan to visit him at the farm in Maryland

where he stood in retirement. Many even sent him birthday cards and flowers. All of this was done to pay tribute to Northern Dancer for his many racing victories, and also for the victories of his children and grandchildren at racetracks around the world.

Chapter One

Family

Northern Dancer enjoying his paddock at Windfields Farm

Northern Dancer was born at 12:15 a.m. on May 27, 1961 at the National Stud Farm (known later as Windfields Farm) in Oshawa, Ontario. While making his late rounds of the barns that night, farm manager Peter Poole sensed that Natalma, the mare who was in foal with Northern Dancer, was about to give birth. Poole had no idea that he was watching history in the making.

Bloodlines

The physical characteristics and temperament of a horse can be traced back to the family tree. The horse's sire (father) and dam (mother) contribute between them about one-half, or 50 per cent, of its total heritage. The four grandparents account for one-quarter, or 25 per cent; the eight great-grandparents pass on one-eighth, or 12.5 per cent, of their traits; and so on down the ancestral line. However, this formula (known as Galton's Law) is not foolproof—sometimes a horse with great bloodlines does not run well at the track, and at other times a horse with humble bloodlines becomes a champion racehorse. Northern Dancer was lucky: he had impressive bloodlines and became a big winner.

Northern Dancer's sire was Nearctic, a stately horse that stood more than sixteen hands tall. At the start of his racing career, Nearctic showed flashes of great promise. As a two-year-old—the youngest that a thoroughbred can race—Nearctic won seven races and was named Canada's top two-year-old racehorse in 1958. Still, there was some disappointment at Windfields Farm. A hoof

Horse Measurements

The height of a horse is not measured in inches and feet, or centimetres and metres, the way it is for humans. Instead, they are measured in units known as "hands." Each hand is equal to four inches, with one-inch increments. The measurement is taken from the ground up to the horse's withers—the highest part of its back, located between the shoulder blades. Any measure less than four inches is written after a decimal; for example, 15.2 hands equals 15 hands and 2 additional inches.

injury had cut Nearctic's racing season short, and his stubborn temperament had cost him races. Nearctic was known for his toughness, and he could be downright disagreeable with the stablehands.

As an older horse, Nearctic became more difficult to ride, and his performances became unpredictable. The numbers at the end of his career—21 wins in 47 races—were good, but not great. Nearctic's owner and trainer believed that the horse could have been better, and even that he *should* have been better— especially considering his advantageous heritage. Nearctic's dam was Lady Angela, a daughter of Hyperion, who was one of Britain's leading sires. Hyperion was of small build and mild temperament, and won several important races such as the Epsom Derby and the St. Leger Stakes. Nearctic was sired by the undefeated Nearco, a great Italian racehorse who was described as one of the most important sires of the 20th century.

Northern Dancer's dam, Natalma, had a few impressive runs as a two-year-old and showed potential in her workouts. But early on it seemed that she lacked just one thing: luck. She ran in only seven races and won three before her career was cut short by a knee injury. Natalma was sent back to Windfields Farm to be bred with Nearctic.

Greatest Racehorses of all Time

At the end of the 20th century, several prestigious publications composed a heavily researched list of their picks of the greatest racehorses of the century in the American arena. *Blood Horse* magazine ranked Native Dancer as 7th overall, with Northern Dancer coming in at 43rd. The *Associated Press* ranked Native Dancer much higher, tied for 3rd with Citation, behind only Man o' War and Secretariat. Northern Dancer did not place.

Northern Dancer's dam, Natalma, at Windfields Farm

Natalma's bloodlines were even more impressive than Nearctic's. Her father was Native Dancer, one of the most famous horses of the early 1950s. Not only did he win all his races as a two-year-old, but he won them "going away"—pulling way ahead of the field of other horses. Known as the Gray Ghost, Native Dancer lost only once — the 1953 Kentucky Derby—in his 22-race career. He won the other two races in the American Triple Crown—the Preakness Stakes and the Belmont Stakes—as well as several other major races, such as the Travers Stakes. Though Native Dancer didn't win the Triple Crown, many experts think he was worthy of it and rank him ahead of winners such as War Admiral, Gallant Fox, and even Sir Barton.

The people at Windfields Farm, knowing the legendary achievements flowing in Northern Dancer's bloodlines, greatly anticipated his birth. But when Northern Dancer was born, he did not seem bold or confident, and he seldom strayed from Natalma's side during the first few weeks of his life. In time he became unruly around his stall, like Nearctic. At least once he ripped the shirt off his trainer.

When Northern Dancer started training, he did not show a gait—a stride or a way of running—that was classically swift or powerful like that of Native Dancer or Nearctic. Many looked at Northern Dancer—short and thick-chested—and thought he'd never make a race-horse, much less a champion. This was the first, but not the last time, that people would underestimate Northern Dancer.

The Millionaire and El Señor

The story of one racehorse's life may seem pretty much the same as any other's. There is some truth to that. But the story of every racehorse—whether it is a horse that never wins a race or a Kentucky Derby champion—starts with people. When a horse like Northern Dancer runs, a lot of people run with him.

The story of Canada's most famous racehorse starts with Edward Plunkett Taylor, the owner of both Windfields Farm and Northern Dancer. E. P. Taylor was born into a wealthy family in Ottawa on January 29, 1901. He was first introduced to the sport of thoroughbred horse racing while he was a student attending McGill University.

In the early 1930s Taylor began to build a financial empire by buying up and merging small, unprofitable breweries to create one large company. At this time, he also started to think about opening a small stable of his own. He bought several racehorses in 1936 and raced them under the name of "Cosgrave Stable" to promote

Cosgrave Brewery, one of the companies he had bought. Laws left over from the Prohibition days did not allow him to advertise his beer. But having a stable that shared the same name as his bestselling brand was one way to sidestep the law. Within a few years, his stable of horses was known across the province, and pictures of his horses featuring the name "Cosgrave" were hung in taverns throughout Ontario.

Taylor wanted to race the horses in his stable, but he was not content with the state of the sport in Canada. He took charge of the Ontario Jockey Club (OJC) in the 1950s, and set about reorganizing it so it could compete with the big horse racing organizations in the United States. Taylor bought all the small racetracks in Ontario, merged them together like he did with his

Woodbine Racetrack

Woodbine was created in 1956 as an improvement to the existing racetracks in Toronto at the time. Completely renovated in 1993, it is one of the few places where thoroughbred racing and harness racing can be held on the same day. It has three tracks, the larger being turf, the middle being synthetic dirt, and the inner being crushed limestone. It hosts major Canadian races, such as the Queens' Plate, the Breeder's Stakes, and the E. P. Taylor Stakes.

small breweries, and built three new racing facilities—
Woodbine, Greenwood, and Fort Erie. Under Taylor's direc-
tion, Ontario racetracks and the OJC soon matched the
standards of leading tracks and operations in the
United States.

But there was still more work to be done. E. P. Taylor
knew that the OJC and his horses would gain respect only
if they achieved success in the biggest
stakes races at the most famous U.S.
tracks. They also had to make an
impression at the yearling sales, where
horse owners and breeders offer their
year-old colts and fillies for sale. When
Taylor started to take his best horses to
the U.S. in the 1950s, American horse
owners and contenders laughed at
him. They told him that his horses
couldn't win any major stakes races in
the States, and that it was too cold and
snowy to raise championship horses in
Canada. Like Northern Dancer, Taylor
wasn't supposed to succeed—but he
wasn't discouraged. He understood
the horse racing business and knew
that he would have to reorganize
Windfields Farm—not just by bringing
in horses with reputable bloodlines,
but also by bringing in one of the best
trainers. And that was Horatio Luro.

Horatio Adolfo Luro—El Señor, as
he was nicknamed at the racetracks—
was born on February 27, 1901, in

Windfields Farm

E. P. Taylor started Windfields
Farm in 1936. He named it
after his first stakes winner,
Windfields. This stable in
Oshawa became an important
landmark for horse racing,
not just because of Northern
Dancer, but because of its
contribution to Canadian
horse racing. Many great
stallions resided at Windfields
Farms, including Windfields
himself, New Providence,
Vice Regent, and, of course,
Northern Dancer.

Horatio Adolfo Luro keeping a watchful eye on Northern Dancer, who is having a rare quiet moment

Buenos Aires, Argentina. He took over his family's horse-breeding establishment, El Moro Stud, in 1933, and brought his first boatload of horses north to the U.S. in 1937. Soon Luro made his mark.

Luro had a great eye and a magic touch. He also had unusual training methods—at least unusual compared to North American methods. In the United States and

Northern Dancer being led from the stud barn at Windfields Farm.

Canada, trainers liked to have their horses run hard
and fast over shorter distances. "I don't agree with the
American trainers," Luro said later when asked about
Northern Dancer's career. "Long gallops are the
European method to develop a classic horse and I think
that is right."

Luro's methods might have been out of the ordinary, but his successes were known throughout the horse-racing community. He came to E. P. Taylor's attention in the mid-1950s, when two of Luro's horses won the Canadian International Stakes: Eugenia II in 1956 and Spinney in 1957.

Taylor sent the then-young filly named Natalma, destined to be Northern Dancer's dam, to the U.S. to train with Luro. One incident in particular made an impression on the trainer. It was something that Luro would later recall when he was training Northern Dancer.

The incident occurred in 1959 at the Spinaway Stakes—a major race for two-year-old fillies—where Natalma was the first to cross the finish line. Immediately after the race, officials at the track posted the "Inquiry" sign, which meant that they were reviewing the race to see if a foul had been committed. The racing officials, or stewards, determined that Natalma had veered into the path of another filly named Warlike and had cost her a fair chance at winning the race. Natalma was penalized and set at third place.

It wasn't the loss of the race that stuck in Luro's mind. What he remembered years later was the *reason* that Natalma had veered off course. In the race, her jockey, Bobby Ussery, had heavily used his whip, and she clearly did not like it. For weeks after the race, Natalma refused to budge from her stall in the barn when it was time for her workouts. She became a different horse. She went from a horse that won stakes races to a horse that didn't want to run at all.

In order to win back her trust, Luro gave Natalma a little vacation around the barn. Eventually, he had her taken out to the track to watch other horses run, and found that, in time, she did not resist when her handlers asked her to run. Soon, Natalma looked ready to pick up where she had left off after what should have been a victory at the Spinaway Stakes.

It turned out that Natalma never raced again. Just a week before her comeback race, she chipped a bone in her knee and had to retire from racing. But Luro always remembered Natalma and, in particular, the way she had reacted to Bobby Ussery's whip. It seemed like a small point with a horse that few people remembered, but it would end up being important in the career of a horse no one would forget.

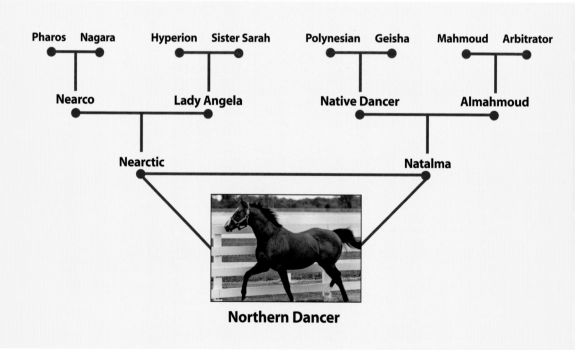

Northern Dancer

Chapter Two

Unwanted Yearling

Northern Dancer, whose potential was not obvious as a yearling

Northern Dancer could have ended up running for an owner who was not E. P. Taylor. He could have ended up being trained by someone who was not Horatio Luro. In fact, Northern Dancer could have left behind a completely different history had fate not intervened.

On September 16, 1962, when he was not even 16 months old, Northern Dancer was put up for sale at Taylor's ninth annual yearling sale. All the major thoroughbred horse owners were invited to Windfields Farm in Oshawa to bid on the stable's yearlings—horses that were born after January 1 of the previous year and would be ready to run in the next racing season.

The handlers at Windfields Farm walked Northern Dancer out in front of the most knowledgeable people in Canadian horse racing. They looked at the horse and at the programs that listed his impressive bloodlines. They knew all about the great Native Dancer.

But when the auctioneer announced that bidding for Northern Dancer would start at $25,000, no one raised a hand. Two other yearlings that day were sold for $25,000, and their names are long forgotten, but there was no bidding on Northern Dancer. Ironically, many years later, Northern Dancer could not be bought for $25 million, $50 million, or even $100 million.

He didn't have the classic look of a great racehorse. He wasn't physically impressive...

Why did the buyers at the auction think so little of Northern Dancer? Because although he had great bloodlines, his looks didn't impress anyone, at least when he was standing still. He didn't have the classic look of a great racehorse. He wasn't physically impressive like Native Dancer, or beautiful like Nearctic and Natalma.

Northern Dancer was easy to pick out among the yearlings, but for all the wrong reasons. He was the shortest, standing just over fourteen hands, meaning he wasn't quite five feet tall. He weighed 955 pounds, which sounds like a lot, but the average yearling weighs about 1,000 pounds. In horse racing, the look and physical make-up

Racetrack Auction

Many of the people who own race-horses do not necessarily breed them on their farms, but buy them at horse auctions, which are held throughout the year. Many prospective buyers come out to see if they can find the next great racehorse. Horses can be sold at all ages, but the most common sale is the yearling sale, where one-year-old horses are sold. Stories of great deals at horse auctions are told in which owners buy a horse for next to nothing, and it ends up becoming a very successful racehorse. The horse Funny Cide was bought at a yearling auction for $22,000 and went on to win over $3.5 million in earnings.

of a horse is called its "conformation," and Northern Dancer's conformation didn't impress anyone at Taylor's yearling sale.

However it wasn't just his conformation that scared off buyers. They knew about Nearctic's inconsistent performances on the track, and about Natalma's injury problems. They feared that Northern Dancer would be destined to follow the career path of Nearctic or Natalma—if the laws of thoroughbred breeding appied. But this was one time the laws wouldn't hold.

Later that month, Northern Dancer and the other unsold yearlings at Windfields Farm began training on Taylor's property in north Toronto. It wasn't long before Taylor and Luro and others around the stables were thankful that Northern Dancer hadn't been sold at the auction.

Even in those first days, it was clear that this young horse wasn't like the others. The colt's temperament was described as "feisty," but never "cuddly," which was not surprising. After all, his dam, Natalma, could be rather nasty in the saddling paddock.

When Northern Dancer started to gallop, he never glided. His gait was like one explosion after another. He could go from standing still to full speed in just a couple of strides. At least once, when Northern Dancer started running, the force of his takeoff threw an experienced rider to the ground. He was, as one of his trainers said, "a wilful son of a gun." He had assets that didn't show in the program at the yearling sale, something that the buyers couldn't pick out when he was paraded in front of them. He had power that they could never have expected in a smaller colt. He also had strength and heart and a competitive nature. There was a lot of Native Dancer in this grandson.

When Northern Dancer was first handed over to Horatio Luro for training, it looked as if El Señor would be no luckier with the son than he had been with the dam, Natalma. In the months before his first race, Northern Dancer was bothered by a cracked heel. A racing career can end if a horse goes lame from an infection that starts out with a cracked heel. So Luro and the others at Windfields Farm had to go very slowly with Northern Dancer.

His injury made it so that Northern Dancer could not run his first official workout until June 1963. The workout at Woodbine Racetrack in Toronto was noted in the *Daily Racing Form*, a newspaper that publishes detailed information about future races and is read by many bettors before they wager. According to its report, Northern Dancer ran three furlongs (one furlong is equivalent to one-eighth of a mile or approximately 200 metres) in just under 40 seconds on a slow track—a very good work-out time.

Less than a month later, Northern Dancer worked out of the mechanical starting gate for the first time. Luro told the practice rider to give him a touch of the whip on the shoulder when the gate opened. The practice rider followed Luro's instruction to the letter, and they were both shocked when Northern Dancer took off as if he'd been shot out of a cannon. He ended up running three furlongs in 37 seconds, just a few seconds off the track record—and he hadn't even competed in a race yet. Two things became clear: first, this colt had real running talent, and second, he didn't like the whip. Northern Dancer would have to be handled carefully.

Horse Injuries

Horse racing is physically strenuous and, as a result, horse injuries are common. The forelegs of a horse are slender but are required to take a lot of weight as they run; therefore, broken bones do occur while racing. Sometimes these injuries can turn deadly if horses cannot recover from their leg injuries, such as Ruffian in 1975 and Barbaro in 2006. Less serious injuries include cracked hooves, like Northern Dancer's injury, inflamed tendons, and strains. Trainers will often err on the side of caution in the case of a less serious injury, since it can cause a misstep on the track and quickly become serious.

In his first race, held at Fort Erie Racetrack, Northern Dancer was already leaving his competitors far behind.

The First Race

Northern Dancer ran his first race at the Fort Erie Racetrack on August 2, 1963. It was a five-and-a-half furlong race for two-year-old maidens (horses still looking for their first win). Eight horses competed for the $2,100 purse.

Northern Dancer's jockey was Ron Turcotte from New Brunswick. "The first time I rode Northern Dancer I knew he was something special," he later said. "He broke sluggishly but laid third most of the way. When I called on him for extra, he moved to the lead immediately but was satisfied to stay head and head with the other horse. As I was instructed not to touch him with the whip, I restrained until we were past the 16th pole, then I decided to disregard orders.

"In order not to be seen by the trainer or assistant trainer, I quickly switched the stick to my left hand and tapped him one time. To my surprise, he exploded. Within 70 yards he opened up an eight-length lead, which is what he won by."

Turcotte figured that if he had gone to the whip earlier—even just a gentle tap—Northern Dancer might have won this short race by fifteen or twenty lengths, an amazing margin of victory.

Turcotte would end up riding two of the most important horses of the era: Northern Dancer as a young jockey and Secretariat as a more experienced rider. In 1973 Turcotte rode Secretariat to victory in the Kentucky Derby in a time that broke Northern Dancer's record, and Secretariat went on to win the Triple Crown. A few seasons later, Turcotte suffered injuries in a horseracing accident that left him in a wheelchair.

> ## Length
>
> A length is a unit of measurement commonly used to describe the distance between horses in a race. It refers to the length of a horse and is equal to approximately eight feet.

Secretariat whispering to his favourite jockey, Ron Turcotte

Chapter Three

Two-Year-Old Stakes Races

Northern Dancer and Ron Turcotte take a moment to revel in breaking his maiden.

I n just one race, Northern Dancer had established himself. Windfields Farm decided to move him immediately into stakes races. Within a couple of weeks of his first easy victory, Northern Dancer was entered in the Vandal Stakes for two-year-olds, again at Fort Erie Racetrack.

Ron Turcotte was already committed to riding Ramblin' Road, so another rider, Paul Bohenko, was brought in for Northern Dancer's first stakes race. Ramblin' Road, a more experienced two-year-old with established track records, won the race, while Northern Dancer got into an early speed duel with Brockton Boy and wore himself out. But even after beating Northern Dancer in the Vandal Stakes, Turcotte knew he had seen something special in the horse. "I was committed to run Ramblin' Road and we won," he said, "but Northern Dancer should have won."

Paul Bohenko was back up on Northern Dancer a week later in the Summer Stakes, a mile race on the turf course at Woodbine Racetrack. The course was wet, and the going was very tough—but Northern Dancer won the race. In just three weeks, he had gone from an untested and underestimated colt to a horse with two victories, including one in a stakes race.

In late September 1963, Windfields Farm entered Northern Dancer in the Cup and Saucer Stakes, a race for Canadian two-year-olds that is slightly over a mile long on the turf course at Woodbine. It is a handicap race, meaning that track officials try to even out the field by giving the better horses more weight—jockey and saddle— to run under. Because of his growing

Track Conditions

One of the peculiarities of horse racing as a sport is the changing track conditions. Tracks can be fast, which refers to a hard, dry surface, or they can be slow, which means that the track is muddy or "sloppy." A slow track is one in which a horse cannot be expected to run as quickly. While some horses do not take well to a slow track, others revel in the mud. This gives them an advantage in some races. Sprinters do not have the endurance to run in mud, but horses that are used to running long distances can handle the extra exertion and run well.

reputation and win in the Summer Stakes, the officials gave Northern Dancer the heaviest weight in the field: 126 pounds.

With Ron Turcotte as his jockey, Northern Dancer led most of the way. But he tired in the late stages of the race and was passed near the finish line by Grand Garçon, a horse that carried the minimum 116 pounds and that bettors gave little chance to win. Northern Dancer lost "by a nose," the narrowest of margins.

Perhaps Northern Dancer's most spectacular run as a two-year-old came in the Bloordale Purse in early October. Again, Northern Dancer was "top weighted," given more weight than the other horses in the field, running under 122 pounds. His Windfields stablemate, Northern Flight, carried 117 pounds, and the rest of the field had even bigger advantages. Northern Flight, another son of Nearctic, sprinted out to a huge lead in the early stages of the race, leading his half-brother by as much as fifteen lengths. For Northern Dancer, it looked like the race was lost. But with Ron Turcotte in the saddle Northern Dancer closed in on Northern Flight and beat him by a length-and-a-half. The next horse was more than twenty lengths behind Northern Flight.

On October 12, 1963, at Woodbine Racetrack, Northern Dancer's short season as a two-year-old on the Ontario Jockey Club tracks was capped by a victory in the Coronation Futurity Stakes, the richest and most prestigious race for Canadian two-year-olds. Grand Garçon also competed and some people, including experts at the *Daily Racing Form*, thought that he would provide a challenge for Northern Dancer. It didn't work out that way. Across a mile and an eighth, Northern

Dancer won by more than six lengths and Grand Garçon finished far back in fifth position. If anyone had doubted that Northern Dancer was the country's best two-year-old, the Coronation Futurity put those doubts to rest.

At this point Windfields Farm was ready to take Northern Dancer to the top U.S. tracks to compete in the late-season stakes races. It was one thing to be the best two-year-old in Canada and another thing to be an early contender for the Kentucky Derby. However, none of the U.S.

Northern Dancer proves himself as the best Canadian two-year-old in the Coronation Futurity Stakes.

races fit into Northern Dancer's schedule until late November. To keep the horse sharp until then, Windfields Farm entered him in the Carleton Stakes at Greenwood Racetrack in Toronto. This seven-furlong race took place on a dirt track in the winds blowing off Lake Ontario. It was another win for Northern Dancer, but not a glorious one, due to the poor conditions.

The less-than-impressive performance at the Carleton Stakes wasn't Northern Dancer's biggest problem. After the race, his handlers found blood around his left front hoof—it was the start of a quarter crack. Unfortunately, this injury would continue to give him trouble, especially during the following races in the United States. But Northern Dancer couldn't stop racing; he could not afford weeks, or maybe even months, off the track if he wanted to make it to the 1964 Kentucky Derby.

To the South of the Border

Northern Dancer's victories in the Sir Gaylord Purse and the Remsen Stakes in New York at the end of November 1963 came at a high cost. The quarter crack had worsened during the races. California blacksmith Bill Bane was brought in to repair the hoof with his "Bane Patch," which was made of the latest polymer materials. It was a daring, almost experimental, treatment but Windfields Farm had to try something different, and it ended up saving Northern Dancer's racing season.

In the early spring of 1964, the horse was shipped to the Hialeah Park Racetrack in Florida for the late-winter "preps." These are the three-year-old stakes races that sort out contenders for the early-summer Triple Crown races. Northern Dancer ran three important races on the Hialeah

The Whip

The riding whip used in horse racing has come under scrutiny, but if used correctly, it causes little pain to the horses. It is used either to urge the horse on, or to keep the horse running straight, as it was used in the 2010 Preakness Stakes with the racehorse Dublin. The whip should be used sparingly and applied to the horse's flanks, a muscular part of the body, to avoid pain. Whips are also commonly waved near the horse's eye in order to get its attention. Some horses, like Northern Dancer, refuse to be whipped, so the whip is only used in serious situations.

Park Racetrack. The first race, a six-furlong dash, wasn't a great success—Northern Dancer was bumped during the race and didn't respond well to being whipped by jockey Bobby Ussery. Luro called the race "a setback," but it was also a lesson for the trainer and the Windfields team. It confirmed Luro's training philosophy—Northern Dancer did not respond well to abuse. "I trained Natalma and you could not abuse her and you could not abuse Northern Dancer," Luro said later. "Ussery punished him to be third and it did not help."

Northern Dancer's next race was a seven-furlong exhibition race (a race where there is no betting). Luro was able to get the world's top jockey, Willie Shoemaker, to

Hialeah Park Racetrack

Hialeah opened to horse racing in 1925 and is still considered one of the most beautiful racetracks in the U.S. Its importance to the world was confirmed in 1979 when it was placed on the National Register of Historic Places. It was a very important track during the winter months from the 1950s to the 1970s, when many famous horses wintered in the area. The park closed to thoroughbred racing in 2001, but now holds quarterhorse racing events.

ride Dancer. Even though Northern Dancer was up against a pair of impressive three-year-olds, Shoemaker guided him to victory in a good time.

A week later, Northern Dancer ran his third race at the Hialeah Park Racetrack—the Flamingo Stakes—ridden again by Shoemaker. In the 1960s, the Flamingo Stakes was the primary "prep" race for the Kentuky Derby in the eastern part of the United States. A victory in the Flamingo Stakes could start trainers, owners, jockeys—and maybe even horses—dreaming about the Kentucky Derby.

Northern Dancer went to the post as the betting favourite in the Flamingo Stakes. Besides his impressive races in New York and his excellent time in the exhibition race a week before, there were two other reasons for the support of the crowd at Hialeah. First, many Canadians on vacation in Florida made their way to the

track. Second, at least half of the people in the stands believed that Willie Shoemaker, who had his pick of the eleven horses in the field, knew something when he chose to ride the Canadian horse.

Northern Dancer easily justified his standing as the race favourite and as a

The winner's circle at Hialeah Park Racetrack, where Northern Dancer had an impressive victory in the Flamingo Stakes

Kentucky Derby contender. He won the race with a decisive two-length victory over Mr. Brick.

Northern Dancer's next race was just five days later at Gulfstream Park. It was a tuneup race—called the Mrs. Florida Purse—for the Florida Derby. Northern Dancer, with Manuel Ycaza in the saddle, won again. The second-place finisher, The Scoundrel, a highly regarded contender for the Kentucky Derby, finished four lengths back, even though he was carrying less weight than Northern Dancer.

Race Preparation

The Kentucky Derby is a crucial test for three-year-old horses. Prep races were designed in order to help them prepare and to be ready. There are several important prep races, such as the Blue Grass Stakes, the Arkansas Derby, and the Rebel Stakes. The Flamingo Stakes that Northern Dancer ran in was an important prep race in his time, but is no longer held.

Northern Dancer destroys the competition in the Mrs. Florida Purse at Gulfstream Park.

E. P. Taylor and Horatio Luro had seen enough in the Flamingo Stakes to justify their belief that they had a Kentucky Derby contender on their hands. But Northern Dancer made the case even clearer with a victory in the final Florida prep, the Florida Derby.

It could have been a disaster. On the day before the race, Northern Dancer's regular exercise boy, the jockey who rode him in workouts, called in sick. His replacement couldn't hold the headstrong colt back. Luro had wanted a light run, but the clockers at the track timed Northern Dancer at a little over 58 seconds for 5 furlongs—better than the race pace. Luro was livid. Could any thoroughbred run the equivalent of two races on two consecutive days?

As it turned out, the only ones hurting after the Florida Derby were those who hadn't bet on the heavily favoured Northern Dancer. With Shoemaker aboard, the outcome of the race was never really in doubt. Northern Dancer again beat The Scoundrel, but in a time that was less impressive than the workout time the day before.

The only people who didn't seem convinced about Northern Dancer were the reporters covering the thoroughbreds for U.S. newspapers and racing journals. Only a writer for *Blood-Horse* magazine came away impressed with Northern Dancer's form in the Florida preps. The reporter joked that The Scoundrel couldn't have caught up to E. P. Taylor's colt "if they had gone around the track twice more."

Many people continued to underestimate Northern Dancer, which was surprising. But even more surprising was the fact that his jockey was one of them.

Chapter Four

Losing "The Shoe"

Willie Shoemaker (right) chats with his competition before a race.

Willie Shoemaker, known as "The Shoe," was the best jockey in the business and the first choice of any trainer. After Northern Dancer's last win in Florida, Shoemaker told Luro that he had decided to ride Hill Rise, a horse from California, in the Kentucky Derby.

"I watched Hill Rise run on several occasions at Santa Anita last winter and was very impressed with him," Shoemaker said. "Northern Dancer is a fine colt and I am deeply grateful to Mr. Taylor and Horatio Luro for the opportunity of having ridden him. However, my instincts tell me that Hill Rise is the better mount for the Derby and I hope I am right."

Other comments by Shoemaker were less diplomatic. "A good big horse can always beat a good little horse," he said. Hill Rise was considerably taller than the short and stout Canadian-bred colt.

It was late to be switching jockeys. Other than Shoemaker, no rider with any experience aboard Northern Dancer had completely satisfied Taylor and Luro. So they decided to seek out someone with a proven record at Churchill Downs, the site of the Kentucky Derby. They approached Bill Hartack, a 31-year-old jockey whose past performances included three Kentucky Derby victories.

In the late 1950s and early 1960s, Bill Hartack was the one rider who was a serious rival to Shoemaker. At that point, they were the only jockeys in U.S. horse racing ever to record 400 wins in a season. But they couldn't have been more different in style. Shoemaker was a patient, stylish, and almost gentle rider. Horses ran for him as if they

Willie Shoemaker

It is ironic that "The Shoe" underestimated Northern Dancer for his size because, throughout his life, that is how people reacted to Willie Shoemaker. Born in 1931, Shoemaker wanted to be an athlete, but it wasn't until he was introduced to horse racing that he found his true calling. He became one of the most famous jockeys in horse racing, particularly for being the oldest jockey to win the Kentucky Derby at age 54.

Bill Hartack poses aboard Northern Dancer after a race.

didn't want to let him down. Hartack, on the other hand, was anything but a classic rider. A memorable description of his style appeared in *Time* magazine: "He scratches all over his mount as if it were a case of hives, endlessly intent on keeping the animal's mind on the work at hand.

He comes down the stretch as though leading a Hollywood cavalry charge." He was also called "the least stylish of successful riders in the history of racing."

Bill Hartack wouldn't commit to riding Northern Dancer in the Kentucky Derby, even after the horse's triumphs in Florida. But he agreed to ride him in the Blue Grass Stakes. This was a tune-up race for Derby contenders at Keeneland Racetrack in Lexington, Kentucky, held in the days leading up to the big race. If things went well in the Blue Grass Stakes, then Hartack would ride Northern Dancer in the Derby. Maybe.

It is hard to know exactly what Hartack had in mind when Northern Dancer and four other horses broke from the gate in the Blue Grass Stakes. There was not much more the jockey could have done to make the race a close one. He held Northern Dancer back while Royal Shuck took the lead at a slow pace. Then, after Northern Dancer got out front, a Kentucky-bred horse, Allen Adair, ran out to the lead. Northern Dancer showed his trademark burst and held on for a narrow victory, but with a time that was three seconds off the track record.

On the eve of the biggest race in thoroughbred racing, Hartack had ridden Northern

Bill Hartack

Born in 1932, Bill Hartack quickly became a well-known name in horse racing. By the age of 27, he had already earned himself a spot in the National Museum of Racing and Hall of Fame. Throughout his lifetime, he and Willie Shoemaker were rivals on the track. Although Shoemaker beat him in the overall number of wins, Hartack was the first jockey to make $3 million in one racing season, and only one of two jockeys to win the Kentucky Derby five times.

Northern Dancer during a workout before one of his big races

Dancer to the least impressive win of his career. This was reason enough for Taylor and Luro to look for another jockey, but there was not enough time. All the top jockeys were committed to other horses.

At the end of April, Northern Dancer arrived at the Churchill Downs track in Louisville. It was a week before the running of the 1964 Kentucky Derby. The colt showed that he was ready to run. Dancer was reeling off impressive workouts, even as his exercise boy tried to hold him back and save his best for the race. Luro saw only good signs in those days before the race.

Though many "railbirds" (long-time regulars at the track) had been talking up The Scoundrel or Hill Rise, there was a lot of interest in Northern Dancer. It wasn't that everyone was finally taking notice of Dancer and giving him the respect he deserved. It was something simpler. Northern Dancer was a good story—from all sorts of angles. He came from Canada, a place that seemed a long way from Kentucky. He didn't look like a champion—he was short and ran with an awkward gait. Hill Rise was the favourite to win, and Northern Dancer was the underdog. Everyone bets on a favourite—and everyone loves an underdog.

Chapter Five

Racing for the Triple Crown

A victorious Northern Dancer draped in the traditional blanket of black-eyed Susans after the Preakness Stakes

O n the day of the Kentucky Derby, a columnist from the *Globe and Mail* covered the race from an unexpected place: the National Stud Farm on the Windfields property near Oshawa, Ontario. Dick Beddoes had decided that he would visit Northern Dancer's home on the day of his biggest race. Beddoes described the scene as "cemetery-quiet," nothing like the atmosphere at Churchill Downs in Kentucky. "Men and boys mucked out stalls same as any other day," he wrote. "Nobody talked about the Derby, except casually, but everyone had a stake in it."

Northern Dancer was running for Taylor, for Luro, and for Hartack. But he was also running for Nearctic, Natalma, and the 25 employees who were working at the National Stud Farm on that first Saturday in May 1964. Less than three years before, they had all been on hand when Natalma gave birth to Northern Dancer, and now

they would stop work for an hour or so to watch the Kentucky Derby televised live from Churchill Downs.

There were twelve horses in the field for the 90th running of the Kentucky Derby, but only two who really captured the imagination of race-goers: Hill Rise and Northern Dancer. The bettors at the track thought Hill Rise was more than twice as likely to win as Northern Dancer. Many bettors backed Hill Rise for the same reason that Shoemaker decided to ride him instead of Northern Dancer—that all things being equal, a good big horse will always beat a good little horse.

Northern Dancer won the 1964 Kentucky Derby by a neck over Hill Rise. The Scoundrel finished third. Northern Dancer set a track record of two minutes for the mile and a quarter—a record that would last until the great Secretariat broke it on a light-ning-fast track in 1973. Even then, Secretariat broke Northern Dancer's time by only three-fifths of a second. The only other horse to beat Northern Dancer's time was Monarchos in 2001.

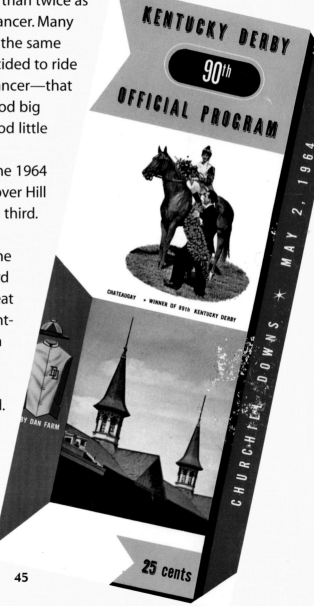

The following is an excerpt from the race summary as it appeared in the *Daily Racing Form*.

> *Northern Dancer*, in good order to gain a contending position along the inside, continued to save ground while under restraint, moved up steadily after six furlongs, but was forced to come out midway of the second turn, responded to gain command a quarter out and prevailed under strong left-handed whipping. *Hill Rise*, unhurried, was bumped twice through the stretch run the first time, continued along the outside thereafter to commence a rally at the half-mile ground, lost additional ground in a wide spread leaving the backstretch, rallied to strong handling on entering the stretch and was slowly getting to the winner. *The Scoundrel* broke in stride, swerved out to bump with

The Kentucky Derby, raced under the twin spires at Churchill Downs, is the most important horse race in the United States.

50 CENTS EVERYWHERE

Copyright under International Copyright Convention. All rights reserved under Pan American Copyright Convention.

TORONTO, ONTARIO, MONDAY, MAY 4, 1964

VOL. XLII. No. 107   654321 T

Northern Dancer Sets Record Winning 90th Kentucky Derby

First Canadian-Bred to Triumph In Famous Classic at Churchill

Mr. and Mrs. E. P. Taylor's Muscular Nearctic Colt Given Perfect Ride by Bill Hartack to Beat Favored Hill Rise By Neck in Mile and Quarter Stepping Distance in 2:00

By JOE HIRSCH

Canada's Great Champion

CHURCHILL DOWNS. Louisville, Ky., May 2.—Sweeping off-the quarter-pole

A newspaper headline heralding Northern Dancer as the winner of the 1964 Kentucky Derby

Hill Rise in the turn to the initial turn, continued in a forward position to gain command between calls on the second turn and weakened gradually through the closing drive.

Thus, it turned out that, in this race, Northern Dancer's size was an advantage. Because he was small and shifty, he managed to stay clear of trouble on the final turn. The larger, longer-striding Hill Rise was bumped and boxed in by the other horses, and required more than one furlong to regain his momentum.

Back at Taylor's National Stud Farm, farm manager Peter Poole jumped high into the air and shouted, "Yippee!" Everyone else, crowded around the television, celebrated with him. They knew that they had lived a dream: They had witnessed the birth and development of a Kentucky Derby champion.

In the days following the race, Shoemaker didn't second-guess his decision to ride Hill Rise. "I had Northern Dancer in a trap in the Derby," the great jockey said. "And when he got out, that was the race. My horse simply didn't have the move in him at the right time. [Hill Rise] is still the best horse."

Perhaps Shoemaker hadn't looked closely at the numbers from the race. Northern Dancer ran the last quarter-mile of the Derby in 24 seconds; faster than he had run the third and fourth quarter-miles of the race. The last horse to finish the race that fast was the 1941 Triple Crown winner Whirlaway.

The Kentucky Derby

Also known as: The Run for the Roses, The Most Exciting Two Minutes in Sports
Distance: A mile and a quarter, or two kilometers
Surface: Dirt
Location: Louisville, Kentucky
Official Song: My Old Kentucky Home
Known for: Elaborate hats.

The Preakness Stakes

After the Kentucky Derby, Northern Dancer was shipped to Pimlico, Maryland, home to the Preakness Stakes, the "second jewel" of the Triple Crown. The Preakness Stakes is the shortest of the Triple Crown races by 110 yards.

Numbers again suggested that Northern Dancer was ready to beat Hill Rise—even more than he had been in the Kentucky Derby. On the day before the race, Luro had a practice rider "blow out"—run at race speed— for Northern Dancer's final three-eights-of-a-mile work-out. His time for the final three-eighths was 35.8 seconds.

Northern Dancer at the wire—or the finish line—of the Preakness Stakes, far ahead of his rivals

It was a burst like his Derby finish, only longer. Hill Rise was given exactly the same workout on the same day by his trainer, Bill Finnegan, but ended up with an entirely different result—and for Finnegan, a disappointing one. Hill Rise ran the last three-eighths of a mile in 40 seconds, more than 4 seconds slower than Northern Dancer.

In the Kentucky Derby, Northern Dancer was part of a field of twelve horses, but he would be facing only five others in the Preakness Stakes, four of them being horses he had beaten in the Derby. There had been a lot of traffic, bumping, and jostling at the Kentucky Derby, something that Hartack had used to his advantage with Northern Dancer, and something that Shoemaker believed had cost Hill Rise a victory. After being bumped and held up in the Derby, Hill Rise had finished only a neck behind Northern Dancer, and Shoemaker was sure

The Preakness Stakes

Also known as: The Run for the Black-Eyed Susans
Distance: A mile and three-sixteenths, or 1.91 kilometres.
Surface: Dirt
Location: Pimlico, Maryland
Official song: Maryland, My Maryland
Known for: The horse and rider weather vane.

that he could get that neck back—and a whole lot more—in the Preakness Stakes.

It didn't work out that way. Northern Dancer won again—this time by more than two lengths—even though Shoemaker was able to run Hill Rise and make his move exactly as he had planned. Hill Rise was not bumped or jostled, but he still finished in third place, just behind The Scoundrel.

Hartack recalled, "We'd been running pretty much together for nearly a quarter mile by the time we hit the stretch. About 50 yards before we reached it I opened up. Hill Rise had been trying to get by me and couldn't. I had a fresh horse and now I let him go. I hit him once halfway around the turn and then we rolled from there. I hand-rode him and hit him left-handed in the stretch. Suddenly Hill Rise was finished. In the last part of the race I could tell my horse was dead tired. But I knew I had the best horse and the fittest, and that if he was tired the horses that were behind us would be even more tired. They weren't going to catch us today."

> **"I could tell my horse was dead tired. But I knew I had the best horse and the fittest..."**
> Bill Hartack

Willie Shoemaker, in turn, sounded regretful about his decision to ride Hill Rise. "Northern Dancer is too much horse," he said. "He's just the best and that's all."

The Belmont Stakes

Next, the top three-year-olds in North America arrived at Aqueduct Racetrack in New York, a temporary location for the Belmont Stakes from 1963 to 1967. During this time, Belmont Park in Elmont, New York, the traditional home of the stakes, was being renovated. After the first two legs of the Triple Crown, Northern Dancer had established himself as the best of the three-year-old racehorses and the favourite to win the Belmont Stakes.

When talking to reporters, E. P. Taylor and Horatio Luro sounded confident about Northern Dancer's chances in

The Belmont Stakes

Also known as: The Run for the Carnations, the Test of the Champion
Distance: A mile and a half, or 2.4 kilometres.
Surface: Dirt
Location: Elmont, New York
Official Song: New York, New York
Known for: The final resting place of the famous filly Ruffian

the Belmont Stakes. "I think he'll be even better at a mile and a half," E. P. Taylor said. "Any speed horse that you can rate has an advantage at this distance provided his jockey is a good judge of pace. We know this horse qualifies and so does Bill Hartack."

Luro disagreed slightly with Taylor but he was still confident that the horse could win the race. "His class, in relationship to the class of the competition, will permit him to run the Belmont distance," Luro said. "The long gallops have tuned his heart perfectly. If we don't make it, it won't be because he's not fit." He also pointed out that the Belmont was going to be Northern Dancer's first race as a true three-year-old.

When Northern Dancer turned three years old on May 27, 1964, friends of E. P. Taylor sent the horse a birthday cake made of carrots and decorated with Canadian flags.

Thoroughbreds' Birthdays

Although thoroughbreds are born anywhere from January to May, the records show them as having their official birthday on January 1. If a thoroughbred was born on December 31, the foal would technically turn one year old the next day! This is not allowed to happen, but it does mean that some horses who are born later in the year end up racing horses that are months older, the way Northern Dancer—born in May—had to do.

The owner received more than 300 cards from well-wishers across North America. It seemed like a fun occasion for Northern Dancer's team, but it was also a reminder that this horse was running ahead of the field. He was the youngest contender at the Triple Crown, still catching up physically, still growing. His best races seemed to be ahead of him.

The 1964 Belmont Stakes was a mighty race—and it was the mightiest disappointment for Taylor, Luro, Hartack, Windfields Farm, Canadian horse-racing fans, and Northern Dancer. Quadrangle, a horse that had finished fifth in the Kentucky Derby and fourth in the Preakness Stakes, won the Belmont at odds of more than six to one. Roman Brother was two lengths behind the winner, and Northern Dancer was a well-beaten third. The result surprised everybody: Quadrangle's trainer hadn't been sure whether he should even enter his horse in the race against Northern Dancer.

Perhaps the result shouldn't have surprised anyone. After all, Quadrangle had great bloodlines, was large, and looked like the classic thoroughbred horse. He had also previously raced five times at Aqueduct, winning four times.

Hartack had assured Luro that although Quadrangle would set the pace, he'd eventually weaken. Northern Dancer, after waiting patiently, would then coast to victory through the final quarter-mile. Quadrangle led as predicted, but his jockey, Manuel Ycaza, took the horse out at a pace that was almost a walk for champion thoroughbreds. Meanwhile, Hartack was wrestling to hold the eager Northern Dancer back. Two things happened when the moment came to give chase: Northern Dancer, his mouth gaping, became completely frustrated, while Quadrangle's stamina which had been saved so carefully allowed him to easily outfinish Roman Brother and Northern Dancer.

"Can't Hartack judge speed? These were fractions for trotting horses," Luro fumed. "Don't blame the horse. He was choked, dying to run."

Always aware that he represented not only his horse but also the Ontario Jockey Club and Canadian horse racing, Taylor tried to be more gracious and diplomatic about the defeat. "Quadrangle ran a fine race. All you have to do is look at his time. We have no excuses today."

Hartack was never diplomatic, and he was especially sour after the Belmont Stakes. "I knew we were in trouble when all the newspapermen picked us to win," Hartack said.

Back in his Belmont stall, Northern Dancer was still coughing up dirt. The Windfields team had suspected that the Belmont Stakes was going to be too demanding for him, and indeed he had been heavily raced. Luro recommended to Taylor that he rest Northern Dancer

Slow Pace

There are two ways to tire out horses in a race. One is to set a fast pace early in the race. The other way is to set a very slow pace. While a slow pace might not sound tiring, horses like Northern Dancer do not like being held back, and will spend their energy fighting the jockey. So even though Northern Dancer was running at a slower pace at the Belmont Stakes, he was being tired out. Meanwhile, Quadrangle, running easily at the front and not fighting his jockey, had enough energy to put on an extra burst of speed at the end.

and save him for races late in the three-year-old season—or even bring him back as a four-year-old. He believed that running a tired horse in any situation was risking injury.

Even though Northern Dancer wasn't as ready for the Belmont as he had been for the Kentucky Derby and the Preakness, Luro went to his grave convinced that a bad ride had cost Northern Dancer the race and the Triple Crown. But Taylor and Luro did not hold it against Hartack when it came time for the Queen's Plate, the Ontario Jockey Club's gala event at Woodbine Racetrack in Toronto. It was fitting, too, that Hartack, who rode Northern Dancer to his most important victories, would also be riding the great colt in the most prestigious race at his home track.

Bad Rides

Hartack's performance in the Belmont Stakes with Northern Dancer was not the first time, nor the last, that a jockey was blamed for a bad race. Willie Shoemaker's ride in the 1957 Kentucky Derby was notorious, and many believe he cost his horse the win. In 2010, Garett Gomez, the jockey of Lookin' at Lucky, was blamed for ruining the colt's chances in both the Santa Anita Derby and the Kentucky Derby. As a result, he was bumped by another rider in the Preakness Stakes.

Chapter Six

Homecoming

Northern Dancer began a new career as a stud upon his retirement from racing.

hen Northern Dancer returned to Toronto from New York on June 8, 1964, he was greeted like a head of state. Dignitaries, reporters, and racing officials waited for him as he was led out of his trailer.

Toronto's mayor, Allan Lamport, named June 8 as Northern Dancer Day in the city. In a ceremony at city hall, Lamport presented Taylor with a key to the city. At his stall, Northern Dancer was given his own copy of the key to the city—it was carved out of a carrot.

Northern Dancer had strained his left foreleg in the Belmont Stakes, an injury that put his entry in the Queen's Plate, Canada's premier race, in question. The seriousness of his injury was kept secret by the Windfields team, but even if it had been public knowledge, Northern Dancer would still have been a heavy favourite at the Queen's Plate on June 20. On the day of the race, one enterprising businessman sold souvenir glasses with engravings of the names of every Queen's Plate winner. Beside the year 1964 was the name "Northern Dancer."

...he was greeted like a head of state. Dignitaries, reporters, and racing officials waited for him...

As the race started, many of Northern Dancer's fans were shaking. They were worried that Canada's greatest-ever thoroughbred might lose the nation's most important race on his home track. Rounding the second turn on the main Woodbine track, Northern Dancer seemed to be boxed in. He was crowded in heavy traffic and unable to move. And he was running dead last.

By the five-eighths pole, Hartack had moved Northern Dancer to the outside of the pack and clear of the field. From there, Northern Dancer sped by the

The Queen's Plate

Also known as: The Gallop for the Guineas

Distance: A mile and a quarter, or two kilometres

Surface: Polytrack (modern day)

Location: Toronto, Ontario

Known for: The oldest North American horse race

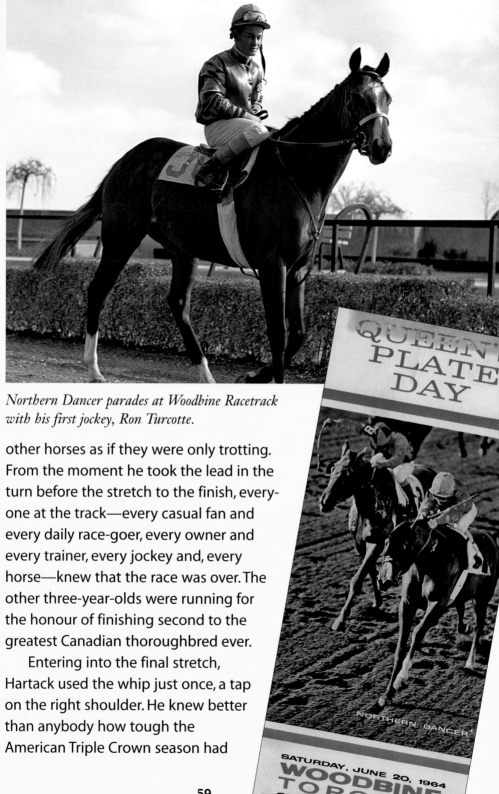

Northern Dancer parades at Woodbine Racetrack with his first jockey, Ron Turcotte.

other horses as if they were only trotting. From the moment he took the lead in the turn before the stretch to the finish, everyone at the track—every casual fan and every daily race-goer, every owner and every trainer, every jockey and, every horse—knew that the race was over. The other three-year-olds were running for the honour of finishing second to the greatest Canadian thoroughbred ever.

Entering into the final stretch, Hartack used the whip just once, a tap on the right shoulder. He knew better than anybody how tough the American Triple Crown season had

QUEEN'S PLATE DAY

NORTHERN DANCER

SATURDAY, JUNE 20, 1964
WOODBINE
TORONTO
OFFICIAL PROGRAM 25¢
PRICE 24¢

been on the colt. He didn't want to take anything more out of Northern Dancer than was necessary to win.

"I knew I had the best horse," Hartack said. "I had so much hold on him I had to keep him from running on top of the others. I tapped him on the shoulder turning for home just to keep his mind on things, but I don't think I [hurt] him. I was easing him up at the finish. It was so easy, never a second when it wasn't simple."

Jerry Harrison, the jockey aboard a horse called All Seasons said, "I couldn't have catched the Dancer if I'd throwed a lasso on him and let him drag me home."

E. P. Taylor congratulates Bill Hartack outside the winner's circle at the Queen's Plate, which was Northern Dancer's last race.

Northern Dancer crossed the line in 2:02.20 minutes, just one-fifth of a second off the race record set by E. P. Taylor's Victoria Park in 1960. If Hartack had asked for anything more from his horse, there is no doubt that Northern Dancer would have broken—even shattered—that record.

The Queen's Plate was barely over when reporters asked Luro what was next for his great three-year-old. Luro talked about future races and talked about getting "revenge" against Quadrangle, the horse that had blocked Northern Dancer's way to the Triple Crown.

The reporters also asked Taylor about his plans for Northern Dancer, and he was a lot more specific than his trainer. "The horse will rest, in a manner of speaking, but no vacation," Taylor said. "He'll gallop two or three miles a day. His next race will be the Travers at Saratoga Springs [a famous track in upstate New York] on August 22."

It was understandable why Taylor wanted his prized thoroughbred to go to Saratoga for the Travers Stakes. It was an historic race—the 1964 race would mark its 100th anniversary. It was also a race made famous by the horses that had won it—legends like Man o' War, Twenty Grand, Whirlaway, and Native Dancer. Northern Dancer had already gained a great name and reputation in racing. Now, Taylor thought, was the time to raise him to the status of a legend.

Taylor went to the winner's circle to accept the winner's share of the Queen's Plate purse, $49,075, as well as the $5,000 gold cup, and 50 guineas, the traditional gift from the British monarch. Northern Dancer arrived in the winner's circle a minute later. He was not as rambunctious as usual. Some people remarked that he almost shied away from photographers. Perhaps the horse knew what the others didn't suspect: that this Queen's Plate was his final race, the final time that horse, rider, and trainer would "combine all their talents into a suave blend."

Chapter Seven

Father of Champions

A painting of Northern Dancer at age 23, during his career as a stud

The tendon that Northern Dancer had injured in the Belmont Stakes had been aggravated in the Queen's Plate. Because of his injury, Northern Dancer did not make it to the Travers Stakes at Saratoga Springs. Months after the Queen's Plate, Windfields Farm announced Northern Dancer's retirement. He had earned $580,000 in eighteen starts, with fourteen wins. That winter he received numerous racing awards and was named Canada's athlete of the year in some polls. He was named the Canadian Horse of the Year and was voted American Champion Three-Year-Old, although he was beaten out for the title of American Horse of the Year by Kelso, a horse that had already won the award a record of four times. It looked like the end of Northern Dancer's story—in fact, it was the end of his first great story, but it was also the beginning of another amazing one.

In retirement, Northern Dancer, like other champion stallions, began a new career as a stud, fathering new generations of champions. He had been underestimated as a yearling and underestimated on the track, but it seemed unlikely that anyone would ever underestimate him again. That, however, is exactly what happened.

> **...named the Canadian Horse of the Year and was voted American Champion Three-Year-Old...**

Many thought that Northern Dancer would make a good sire but not a great one. These doubters said that his loss in the Belmont Stakes was a sign that his sons and daughters would be sprinters, rather than horses that could run well across longer distances.

In his first year at stud, Northern Dancer sired Viceregal, the undefeated two-year-old Canadian champion and Horse of the Year in 1968. The next year, he sired Nijinsky II, his first European champion. Nijinsky II is as respected and remembered in Great Britain—which has horse-racing traditions older and richer than those in North America—as Northern Dancer is in Canada.

Viceregal and Nijinsky II were the first of many. After them came The Minstrel, Sadler's Wells, Nureyev, Storm

Bird, Lyphard, Vice Regent, El Gran Señor, Secreto, Shareef Dancer, Fanfreluche, Lauries Dancer, and Northernette— all champions. Of the twenty-one horses Northern Dancer sired in 1966, eighteen ran races and ten won stakes

Famous Descendants

Northern Dancer's bloodline has had such a profound effect that it has spanned the globe and influenced his many descendants from his children, all the way downto his great-great-grandchildren.

Famous Sons around the World:

Canada: **Viceregal** (1966) Canadian Horse of the Year

England: **Nijinsky II** (1967) Voted the Horse of the Millennium by the British Newspaper, *The Sun*.

France: **Lyphard** (1969) Best known as a sire

Ireland: **Storm Bird** (1978) Two-year-old Champion in England and Ireland

Japan: **Northern Taste** (1971) Winner of many European races including Prix Djabel

United States: **Danzig** (1977) Injuries ended his racing career early but was successful as a stud

Famous Daughters:

Fanfreluche (1967), who was named American Champion Three-Year-Old Filly in 1970. She was kidnapped in June 1977, but was found five months later.

Lauries Dancer (1968) earned the honour of Canadian Horse of the Year in 1971 and was inducted into the Canadian Horse Racing Hall of Fame in 2006.

Northernette (1974), full sister of Storm Bird, was the 1977 Canadian Champion Three-Year-Old Filly and was also inducted into the Canadian Horse Racing Hall of Fame.

Famous Grandchildren:

Storm Cat (1983) grandson, was the leading sire in North America in 1999 and 2000.

Deputy Minister (1979), grandson, was named the 1981 North American Champion Two-Year-Old and was inducted into the Canadian Horse Racing Hall of Fame in 1988.

Dance Smartly (1988), granddaughter, was the winner of the 1991 Canadian Triple Crown and earned more money than any other filly in the world at the time.

Famous Great-grandchildren:

Charismatic (1996), the 1999 Horse of the Year, and **Cat Thief** (1996), winner of the 1999 Breeders' Cup Classic, were rival great-grand sons who went up against each other in the 1999 Triple Crown.

Monarchos (1998), great-grandson, won the 2001 Kentucky Derby and became the second and only other horse to beat Northern Dancer's time.

Open Mind (1986), Great-granddaughter who won the 1989 American Triple Tiara (female equivalent to the Triple Crown).

Go for Wand (1987), Ranked 72nd in *Blood-Horse* magazine's list of greatest race horses of the century.

Famous Great-great-grandchildren:

Mine that Bird (2006), the 2009 Kentucky Derby winner, and **Summer Bird** (2006), who won the 2009 Belmont Stakes, were great-great-grandsons who had Northern Dancer on both sides of their pedigree.

Curlin (2004), great-great-grandson, won the 2007 Preakness Stakes and was Horse of the Year for two years in a row.

Silverbulletday (1996), great-great-granddaughter of Northern dancer, was honoured with the titles of American Champion Two-Year-Old Filly in 1998 and American Champion Three-Year-Old Filly in 1999.

In 2007, great-great-granddaughter **Rags to Riches** (2004) was the first filly to win the Belmont Stakes since 1905.

Rachel Alexandra (2006), the 2009 Horse of the Year, had Northern Dancer as a great-great-grand-father on both sides of her pedigree.

races—an amazing number. Northern Dancer was named North America's leading sire in 1971 and 1977, and leading sire in England in 1970, 1977, 1983, and 1984.

The successes of Northern Dancer's sons and daughters didn't just win honours for Taylor and Windfields Farm. Northern Dancer also brought in millions of dollars. His bloodline became so intensely sought after that his stud fee skyrocketed from $25,000 in 1971 to over $1 million in the early 1980s. His yearlings sold for an average of over $1 million in 1981, and in 1984 his fourteen yearlings sold for an average of $3.3 million, a record that might never be surpassed. Furthermore, a yearling sold for the record price of $10.2 million in 1983, and in the next year, one of his grandsons went for $13.1 million. Northern Dancer fathered 146 stakes winners and innumerable champions on four continents. It may be difficult to add up all the dollars, but if his sons and daughters, and his grandsons and granddaughters are counted, it may be that Northern Dancer generated over a billion dollars. And late in Northern Dancer's life, at the elderly age of 21, a French syndicate offered to buy him for $40 million. Taylor turned the offer down— Northern Dancer would stay at Windfields with the people he had known all his life.

> **"He was the greatest commercial stallion ever."**
>
> Joe Hickey

"The old horse might be gone, but he sure put his stamp on the breed," said Joe Hickey, former manager of Windfields Farm, who managed Northern Dancer's stud career. "He was the greatest commercial stallion ever. They'll be selling horses for a lot of years, but they'll never get the prices Northern Dancer did. His impact was felt worldwide."

***

In 1987, at the age of 26, Northern Dancer
retired from stud duty. Three years later, after
suffering from colic and heart problems,
Canada's greatest racehorse died. "It was
remarkable he beat the odds as long as he
did," said Joe Hickey. Northern Dancer was buried at
Windfields Farm, where he had been born 29 years before.

After Northern Dancer's death, so many tributes
poured in that it seemed as if a head of state, rather than a
horse, had died. The best tribute to Northern Dancer captured not only his career on the track, but also his lasting
influence on thoroughbred racing. It came from John
Eisenberg of the *Baltimore Sun*: "It was a spectacular life.
No other description does justice to Northern Dancer's
29 years. The amount of money traded in his name, his

Timeline

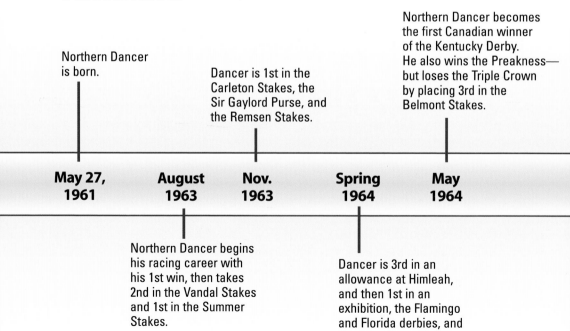

Northern Dancer becomes
the first Canadian winner
of the Kentucky Derby.
He also wins the Preakness—
but loses the Triple Crown
by placing 3rd in the
Belmont Stakes.

Northern Dancer
is born.

Dancer is 1st in the
Carleton Stakes, the
Sir Gaylord Purse, and
the Remsen Stakes.

**May 27,
1961** **August
1963** **Nov.
1963** **Spring
1964** **May
1964**

Northern Dancer begins
his racing career with
his 1st win, then takes
2nd in the Vandal Stakes
and 1st in the Summer
Stakes.

Dancer is 3rd in an
allowance at Himleah,
and then 1st in an
exhibition, the Flamingo
and Florida derbies, and
the Blue Grass Stakes.

brilliant record as a stallion long after he should have died, the little body that accompanied his big name—you could write it all down and call it a true story, and only those who knew it was true would believe it."

***

A vast number of quality horses can trace their bloodlines back to Northern Dancer. In 1992, Northern Park, one of the last two colts sired by Northern Dancer, won a stakes race in France—giving Northern Dancer the honour of having sired 146 stakes winners. Until then, he had been tied with his son Nijinsky II for the record of 145 stakes winners. Today, the record for siring stakes winners is held by Northern Dancer's son Danzig with 186 stakes winners.

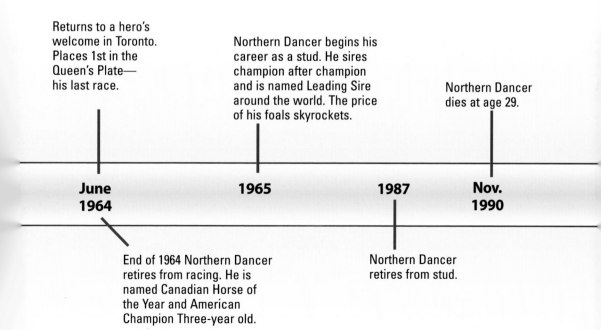

Returns to a hero's welcome in Toronto. Places 1st in the Queen's Plate—his last race.

Northern Dancer begins his career as a stud. He sires champion after champion and is named Leading Sire around the world. The price of his foals skyrockets.

Northern Dancer dies at age 29.

June 1964

1965

1987

Nov. 1990

End of 1964 Northern Dancer retires from racing. He is named Canadian Horse of the Year and American Champion Three-year old.

Northern Dancer retires from stud.

Northern Dancer's influence is felt not only in Canada and the United States but also around the world. Northern Park might have been the last son of Northern Dancer to win a stakes race, but in France the great Canadian horse remains a presence. In 2009, all nineteen of the starters in Europe's most famous race, the Prix de l'Arc de Triomphe at Longchamp, carried Northern Dancer's blood in their veins.

Northern Dancer's true legacy is in his impact on horse racing, which continues long after his death. Although he was not listed as the greatest racehorse of the century, no other horse has affected the sport as much as Northern Dancer has. Within the past twenty years of the American and Canadian Triple Crowns, Northern Dancer's direct descendants have won eleven Kentucky Derby races, sixteen Queen's Plates, fifteen Preakness Stakes, eighteen Prince of Wales Stakes, sixteen Belmont Stakes and nineteen Breeders' Stakes. Four of the five Canadian Triple Crown winners since Northern Dancer have been his offspring. Northern Dancer's bloodline continues to dominate the top honours in horse racing, and his legacy lives on in his descendants.

Glossary

Bane Patch: a treatment for quarter cracks using polymer materials, developed by Californian blacksmith Bill Bane

blow out: run at race speed

by a nose: by an extremely slim margin (literally, the horse's "nose" is the only thing ahead of the second horse)

conformation: the look and physical make-up of a horse. Conformation is usually judged by the intended use of the animal (the best conformation for a racing horse is different from the best conformation for a show jumping horse).

dam: mother

field: 1. all of the horses participating in a race; 2. a particular group of horses within a race

furlong: a measure of distance commonly used in horse racing. A furlong is equal to 220 yards, which is 1/8th of a mile or about 201 metres.

gait: the way in which a horse moves. The four most common horse gaits (in order of slowest to fastest) are the walk, trot, canter, and gallop.

going away: winning while increasing one's lead over the other horses

hand: equal to four inches; the standard measurement for horses, taken from the ground to the withers (where the neck joins the body, a high point located between the shoulder blades). Any measure less than four inches is written as a decimal; for exam-ple, 15.2 hands equal 15 hands and 2 addi-tional inches (for a total of 62 inches).

"Inquiry" sign: posted if the outcome of the race is being investigated; this occurs when something has happened during the race that may have unfairly affected a horse's final placing (such as one horse bumping another)

leg: one event that makes up part of a greater whole. For example, the Kentucky Derby is the first leg of the U.S. Triple Crown.

length: a unit of measurement commonly used to describe the distance between hors-es in a race. It refers to the length of a horse and is approximately equal to 8 ft or 2.4 m.

maiden: a horse that has yet to win its first race

preps or "prep races": these are stakes races that help prepare a horse for a significant race. In the case of the Kentucky Derby, preps usually begin in January and end in April. These races also help owners and trainers decide if their horse is good enough to race in a particular event.

quarter crack: a common source of lame-ness in racehorses. Quarter cracks usually start at the top of the hoof (the coronet, or "coronary" band) and run downward at an angle.

railbirds: long-time regular spectators at the track. They usually watch from behind the rail at track level.

sire: father

sloppy: wet or muddy track conditions. Generally, a sloppy track is a slow track and not all horses run well on this surface consistency.

stakes races: races in which horse owners have (usually) paid an entrance fee to participate

stewards: horse racing officials

stud: a horse whose main job is to sire other horses

thoroughbred: a specific breed of horses, to which all racehorses belong, originally developed in England by crossing Arabian stallions with European mares.

top weighted: given more weight to carry than the other horses running in a particular race

Triple Crown: the "Triple Crown of Thorough-bred Racing"; countries who have established thoroughbred racing programs usually have their own Triple Crown series (consisting of three races). Northern Dancer ran in all three legs of the United States Triple Crown and the first leg of the Canadian Triple Crown.

American Triple Crown (or United States Triple Crown): consists of three thorough-bred horse races that take place annually in the United States: the Kentucky Derby, the Preakness Stakes, and the Belmont Stakes. A horse only wins the Triple Crown if it wins all three races, and only three-year olds are allowed to compete.

Canadian Triple Crown: consists of three thoroughbred horse races that take place annually in Canada: the Queen's Plate (run at Woodbine Racetrack, in Toronto, Ontario), Prince of Wales Stakes (run at Fort Erie Racetrack, in Fort Erie, Ontario), and the Breeder's Stakes (run on turf at Woodbine Racetrack, in Toronto, Ontario). A horse only wins the Triple Crown if it wins all three races, and only three-year olds are allowed to compete.

trot: a two-beat gait; faster than walking, slower than cantering

turf: a type of racetrack surface consisting of matted grass

Index

Image Credits

pg. 7 — photo courtesy of Michael Burns Photography

pg. 9 — mural of Northern Dancer's life painted by David Yeats, reproduced with permission

pg. 9 — stamp portrait of Northern Dancer, copyright courtesy of Canada Post Corporation, 1999; reproduced with permission

pg. 10 — photo courtesy of Michael Burns Photography

pg. 13 — photo courtesy of Michael Burns Photography

pg. 15 — photo courtesy of Debbie Kerkhof

pg. 16 — from the collection of Louis Caz

pg. 17 — photo courtesy of Michael Burns Photography

pg. 18 — from the collection of Louis Caz, copyright courtesy of The Drummer Boy

pg. 20 — photo courtesy of Michael Burns Photography

pg. 21 — photo courtesy of Michael Burns Photography

pg. 23 — photo courtesy of Debbie Kerkhof

pg. 26 — photo courtesy of Michael Burns Photography

pg. 27 — photo copyright by Corbis Images

pg. 28 — photo courtesy of Michael Burns Photography

pg. 31 — photo courtesy of Michael Burns Photography

pg. 34 — from the collection of Louis Caz

pg. 35 — from the collection of Louis Caz

pg. 37 — photo copyright by Corbis Images

pg. 39 — photo courtesy of Michael Burns Photography

pg. 41 — from the collection of Louis Caz

pg. 43 — photo courtesy of Jim McCue
pg. 44 — photo copyright by Corbis Images

pg. 45 — from the collection of Louis Caz

pg. 46 — photo courtesy of Michael Burns Photography

pg. 47 — photo courtesy of Michael Burns Photography

pg. 48 Northern Dancer newspaper clipping— copyright courtesy of McMurray Publishing Co. Ltd (Fort Erie and Mohawk Raceway Past Performances Daily Racing Form Vol. XLII. No.107 654321T Toronto, Ontario; May 4, 1964)

pgs. 50–51 — photo courtesy of Jim McCue

pg. 53 — photo courtesy of Michael Burns Photography

pg. 57 — photo courtesy of Michael Burns Photography

pg. 59 — photo courtesy of Michael Burns Photography

pg. 59 — from the collection of Louis Caz

pg. 60 — photo courtesy of Michael Burns Photography

pg. 62 — painting by Anthony M. Alonso, reproduced with permission

pg. 66 — photo copyright courtesy of Danielle Tate-Stratton